Tokyo Metropolitan Theatre

Tokyo Metropolitan Theatre and Sol
in association with NODA MAP pres

THE BEE

by Hideki Noda and Colin Teevan

based on the original story *Mushiriai* (*Plucking At Each Other*)
by Yasutaka Tsutsui

The Bee was first presented by Soho Theatre and NODA MAP
and had its premiere at Soho Theatre, London, 21 June 2006

The Bee in 2006 was supported by the Harold Hyam Wingate
Foundation, The Paul Hamlyn Foundation, The Japan Foundation
through the Performing Arts JAPAN Programme, by the Agency for
Cultural Affairs, Government of Japan, and by Asahi Beer.

Supported by
**ARTS COUNCIL
ENGLAND**

Soho Theatre is a charity
registered in England and Wales No.267234

Tokyo Metropolitan Theatre and Soho Theatre in association
with NODA MAP present the 2012 world tour of

The Bee

by Hideki Noda and Colin Teevan

based on the original story *Mushiriai (Plucking At Each Other)*
by Yasutaka Tsutsui

Kathryn Hunter	**Ido**
Glyn Pritchard	**Anchoku, Ogoro, Ogoro's Son, Reporter**
Clive Mendus	**Dodoyama, King of Chefs, Reporter**
	(For New York and London)
Marcello Magni	**Dodoyama, King of Chefs, Reporter**
	(For Hong Kong and Tokyo)
Hideki Noda	**Ogoro's Wife, Reporter**
Director	**Hideki Noda**
Designer for New York,	**Miriam Buether**
London, and Tokyo	
Designer for Hong Kong	**Yukio Horio**
Lighting Designer (Original)	**Rick Fisher**
Lighting Designer	**Christoph Wagner**
for Hong Kong	
Sound Designer	**Paul Arditti**
Visual Planner	**Shutaro Oku**
for Hong Kong	
Production Stage Manager	**Nick Ferguson**
Technical Stage Manager	**Nick Hill**
Deputy Stage Manager	**Rebecca James**
Assistant Stage Manager	**Kate Wilson**
Sound Engineer	**Chris Reid**
Costume Supervisor	**Chris Cahill**
Props Supervisor	**Sarah Buik**
Assistant to the Director	**Ragga Dahl Johansen**
Artist Coordinator	**Susan Momoko Hingley**
Set built by	**Capital Scenery Ltd. UK.**

The Bee Tour 2012

January 5-15, 2012	Japan Society as part of Under The Radar Festival, New York
January 24-February 11, 2012	Soho Theatre, London
February 17-19, 2012	Hong Kong Arts Festival, Hong Kong
February 24-March 11, 2012	Suitengu Pit, Tokyo (Tokyo Metropolitan Theatre)

Hideki Noda

Co-writer/Director/Ogoro's Wife/Reporter

Hideki Noda is a prolific writer, director, and actor. He became the artistic director of Tokyo Metropolitan Theatre as of July 2009. His work has had a huge influence on Japanese Theatre, and he has long been acclaimed as a leading theatre practitioner.

Hideki launched his first theatre company, Yume no Yuminsha (Dreaming Bohemian) whilst at the University of Tokyo in 1976, creating many works to much acclaim. He went on to study theatre in London and, in 1993, established the theatre production company called NODA MAP. Hideki's recent theatre credits as writer/director/actor include *The Bee* (Japan/Soho Theatre, London),

Red Demon (Japan/Young Vic, London/Thailand/Korea), *The Diver* (Japan/Soho Theatre, London), *Descent of the Brutes* (Japan/Edinburgh Lyceum Theatre), *A Messenger from the Comet* (BAM, New York/Japan), *The Character* (Japan), and *South* (Japan).

In collaboration with the Kabuki actor Nakamura Kanzaburo XVIII, he has adapted Kabuki plays and directed productions such as *Tragedy of Togitatsu* and *Nezumi Kozo* (his original versions of the classical Kabuki piece at Kabuki Theatre), *The Opera Macbeth* (New National Theatre, Japan). Hideki is also actively involved in international productions. He has won most of the major drama awards in Japan. He was appointed an Honorary Officer of the British Empire (OBE) in October 2009 and the Medal with Purple Ribbon (for contributions to education and culture) in June 2011.

Writer

Colin Teevan *Co-writer*

Colin Teevan's recent stage work includes: *There Was a Man, There Was No Man* and *The Lion of Kabul* as part of *The Bomb* and *The Great Game* seasons respectively (Tricycle Theatre, London) *How Many Miles to Basra?* (winner of 2007 Clarion Award for Best New Play), *The Diver* and *The Bee*, both co-written with Hideki Noda. *Missing Persons; Four Tragedies and Roy Keane* and *Monkey!* (The Young Vic), *The Walls*, (National Theatre, London). Adaptations include *Kafka's Monkey* (Young Vic), *Peer Gynt*, (National Theatre Scotland and Barbican Theatre), *Don Quixote* with Pablo Ley and *Svejk* (Gate Theatre/TFANA, NY). Translations include: Euripides' *Bacchai* (National Theatre, London) and Manfridi's *Cuckoos* (Barbican, London) both directed by Sir Peter Hall; *Marathon* by Edoardo Erba (Gate London) and *Iph...* after Euripides (Lyric, Belfast). Television includes *Single Handed* and *Vera* for ITV, and forthcoming political trilogy for RTE and Touchpaper TV. Colin has written over 20 plays for BBC Radio and is currently senior lecturer in Creative Writing at Birkbeck College, University of London. All his work is published by Oberon Books.

Cast

Kathryn Hunter *Ido*

Theatre credits include: *Kafka's Monkey – Solo* (Young Vic); *King Lear – The Fool* (RSC); *Antony & Cleopatra – title role* (RSC); *Fragments* (Young Vic, Bouffes du Nord & World Tour); *The Bee* (Soho); *Whistling Psyche* (Almeida Theatre); *Richard III – title role* and *The Taming of the Shrew – Katarina* (Globe); *King Lear – title role* (Leicester, Tokyo, Globe); *Electra* (Leicester); *Spoonface Steinberg – solo* (Ambassadors, Washington); *Mother Courage – title role* (Ambassadors, Spoletto Festival); *Pericles* and *The Visit* (Complicite, National) (Olivier Award for Best Actress 1990). As Director: *Othello* (RSC); *The Birds* (National); *Mr Puntila and his Man Matti* (Almeida, Albery, Traverse); *The Glory of Living* (Royal Court); *Comedy of Errors* and *Pericles* (The Globe). Film/ Television includes: *Harry Potter & The Order of the Phoenix, All or Nothing, Wet and Dry, Orlando, Baby of Macon, Rome, Silent Witness.*

Glyn Pritchard *Anchoku/Ogoro/ Ogoro's Son/Reporter*

Glyn trained at the, Webber Douglas Academy, London. Theatre credits include: *The Dark Philosophers* (National Theatre Wales/Told by an Idiot), *The Black Album, Fuente Ovehuna, Ghetto* (National Theatre), *Othello* (RSC), *The Bee, The Diver* (Noda Map/Soho Theatre), *A Family Affair* (Arcola Theatre), *Under Milk Wood* (Tricycle Theatre), *Accidental Death of an Anarchist, Hard Times* (Theatre Clwyd), *A Christmas Carol* (Dukes Theatre), *Body Talk* (Royal Court Theatre) T.V. credits include: *Brookside, The Indian Doctor, Coronation Street, A Mind To Kill, Pobol Y Cwm.* Film credits include: *Hunky Dori, Butterflies, Weekenders, Death of A Son, The Last Minute, Lion.*

Clive Mendus *Dodoyama/King of Chefs/Reporter* (New York, London)

Clive is a creature of the theatre and has spent over thirty years touring in the UK and internationally. This is Clive's second collaboration with Hideki Noda, having acted previously in *Red Demon* at the Young Vic, London. He has collaborated most of his working life with Complicite. The shows with Complicite are: *The Street of Crocodiles, The Visit, Help I'm Alive, Caucasian Chalk Circle*, and later this year *The Master and Margarita*. Clive has worked for the Royal Shakespeare Co. acting in *Othello* (directed by Kathryn Hunter), and movement directing on *The Comedy of Errors*. Clive also works as a movement director, currently *The 39 Steps* in London and has worked on *A Respectable Wedding* (Young Vic).

Marcello Magni *Dodoyama/King of Chefs/Reporter* (Hong Kong, Tokyo)

Marcello is an actor, director, movement director from Bergamo, Italy, graduated from Ecole Jacques Lecoq, leads workshops internationally, and has studied with Pierre Byland, Philippe Gaulier and Monica Pagneux. Co-Founder of Complicite in London in 1983. He worked with the company for over twenty-five years. Performed in *A Minute Too Late, Help I'm Alive, The Visit, The Winter's Tale, Street of Crocodiles* and the opera *A Dog's Heart*. Marcello worked in *the Merchant of Venice, Comedy of Errors* and *Pericles* at Shakespeare's Globe, Hideki Noda in *Red Demon*, performed the Fool in *King Lear, The Rose Tattoo, Mother Courage, The Game of Love and Chance* and *The Birds*. In 2006 he performed in *Fragments*, directed by Peter Brook at Théâtre des Bouffes du Nord, Paris and world tour and in *A Magic Flute* by Peter Brook in 2010. Recently he directed and performed in *Tell Them That I am Young and Beautiful* at the Arcola Theatre, London and performed in Italy his solo show *Arlecchino*, originally created at BAC London. Films include: *Nine, The Adventures of Pinocchio, Doctor Who*. Marcello is the voice of *Pingu*.

Company

Miriam Buether *Designer* (New York, London, and Tokyo)

Design credits for theatre/dance/opera include: *The Government Inspector, The Good Soul Of Szechuan, Generations* (Young Vic); *Decade, Earthquakes in London, Six Characters in Search of an Author* (Headlong Theatre); *Sucker Punch, Cock* (Royal Court Theatre); *Cinderella* (Göteborg Ballet); *Tenderhooks* (Canadian National Ballet); *Guantanamo: Honor Bound to Defend Freedom* (Tricycle Theatre, West End and transfers New York and San Francisco); *Anna Nicole, Il Trittico* (Royal Opera House); *Turandot* (English National Opera). She was the overall winner of the 1999 Linbury Prize and she won the Evening Standard Award 2010 for Best Design for *Earthquakes in London* and *Sucker Punch*.

Yukio Horio *Set Designer* (Hong Kong)

Yukio Horio graduated from Musashino Art University, Tokyo, Japan. While he studied at Musashino Art University, Horio went to Germany, and studied stage art at the Staatliche Hochschule für Bildende Künste, Berlin, from 1969 to 1971. His previous theatre productions include: *Kinshuu* (Written and directed by John Caird), and *Steam from an Invisible Man* (Written and directed by Hideki Noda). Musicals include: *Elisabeth*, and *Mozart!*. Opera productions include: *Macbeth*

(Directed by Hideki Noda) and *Der fliegende Holländer* (New National Theatre). He won the Yomiuri Theater Award for the Best Staff in 1996 and 1999, Kisaku Ito Award for Outstanding Achievement in Theatre Arts in 1991, Kinokuniya Theatre Award in 2000, and the 7th Asahi Performing Arts Award for the Best Staff in 2007.

Rick Fisher *Lighting Designer* (Original)

Born in Philadelphia, Rick is based in the UK and winner of two Olivier Awards for Best Lighting Design and two Tony and Drama Desk Awards for *Billy Elliot* and *An Inspector Calls* (Broadway). Previous work for Noda Map: *Red Demon* (London, Tokyo); *The Bee* (London). Theatre work currently running: *Billy Elliot, the Musical* (West End/Australia/Broadway/US Tours); *An Inspector Calls* (UK tour). Recent opera productions include: *Salomé* (Saito Kinen Festival), numerous operas for English National Opera, Royal Opera House and Santa Fe Opera. Dance includes: *Matthew Bourne's Swan Lake* (London/Los Angeles/Broadway/World Tour).

Christoph Wagner *Lighting Designer* (Hong Kong) *Lighting based on original design by Rick Fisher*

Christoph Wagner trained at Queen Margaret University College, Edinburgh. Recent design credits include *Etherdome* (Jackson's Lane Theatre, touring),

Verona Road (Intermission Theatre), *Miss Lily Gets Boned* (Finborough Theatre) and *The Missionary's Position* (Hoxton Hall, touring). Designs for Soho Theatre, where he was Head of Lighting for many years, include: *Everything Must Go, The Diver* (also at Theatre Tram, Japan), *The Tiger Lillies – Seven Deadly Sins, Moonwalking in Chinatown, Thom Pain (based on nothing), How to Act Around Cops, How To Lose Friends And Alienate People* and numerous cabaret and comedy shows.
www.christophwagner.co.uk

Paul Arditti *Sound Designer*

Recent work includes Damon Albarn's new opera *Dr. Dee* at Manchester International Festival; *The Veil, Collaborators, One Man, Two Guvnors, London Road*, all at the National Theatre, London; *Jumpy* at the Royal Court, London; The Pet Shop Boys' ballet *The Most Incredible Thing* at Sadler's Wells, London; *Company* at the Crucible, Sheffield. Awards for sound design include a Tony Award, Olivier Award, Drama Desk Award and BroadwayWorld.com Fans' Choice Award for the sound design of *Billy Elliot, the Musical*; Olivier Award for *Saint Joan* at the NT; Drama Desk Award for *The Pillowman* on Broadway; Evening Standard Award for *Festen* in the West End.
www.paularditti.com

Shutaro Oku *Visual Planner*
(Hong Kong)

Film director / Visual planner.
Shutaro Oku was awarded
'special mention' at Seoul Film
Festival in 2002 with his maiden
work *KAI-ON*. Since then he
has produced a series of films
constantly, such as *Labor Cop,
Japanese Naked Tribe*, and *Aka-
sen*. He has been officially invited
by worldwide film festivals since
the first invitation from Berlin
International Film Festival in 2006
with his work *Cain's Descendant*.
As a stage visual planner, Oku
has directed *Elisabeth* for Toho
Musicals, *The Character* for
NODA MAP and *Casablanca*
for Takarazuka, etc. After his
good use of videos/visuals in
*TAP MANxPIANO MANxMOVIE
MAN*, and *Yoshida Brothers
Live*, he was highly praised for
his originality and possibility
in *Black Cat* and received
'Excellent Staff Award' at Yomiuri
Theater Awards in 2008. Since
then, in addition to his works
Kimidori, Freaks, and *South of
Heaven*, Oku has been directing
treatre works constantly full of
originality.
www.okushutaro.com

東京芸術劇場

Tokyo
Metropolitan
Theatre

Tokyo Metropolitan Theatre (TMT)

Tokyo Metropolitan Theatre (TMT) opened in October 1990, with the objective of providing a venue for the further development of art and culture for the citizens of Tokyo, and providing a platform for international exchange opportunities. TMT is an arts and culture complex, with multiple facilities that can be rented by the public.

As a unique facility for the performing arts that is operated by the Tokyo Metropolitan Foundation for History and Culture, and supported by the city of Tokyo, TMT is in the process of drastically transforming itself. In July 2009, Hideki Noda, a prominent playwright, director, and actor, was appointed as the first artistic director of Tokyo Metropolitan Theatre to enhance its programmes mainly in the field of theatre. Recently, TMT is becoming more involved in planning and producing performances on its own. It engages outstanding artists and artistic entities to work collaboratively with the theatre.

TMT productions include; *The Diver* (written and directed by Hideki Noda, 2009), *Nogyo Shoujo* (*Girl of the Soil*, written by Hideki Noda, directed by Suzuki Matsuo, 2010), *Chekhov?!* (directed by Kuro Tanino, 2011), Japan-Thai collaboration project *Red Demon Thai Likay version* and Thai adaptation of *Girl of Soil* (2009). TMT also presents 'Geigeki Eyes' series which introduce the productions of emerging playwrights and theatre companies of younger generations, such as Hideto Iwai (hi-bye), Fai Fai, and Kaki-Kuu-Kyaku.

TMT presents foreign productions as well, such as British theatre company Propeller's *A Midsummer Night's Dream* and *The Merchant of Venice* (directed by Edward Hall, 2009), and *Blue Dragon* (directed by Robert Lepage, 2010).

Tokyo Metropolitan Theatre

Artistic Director	**Hideki Noda**
Director	**Shigeo Fukuchi**
Vice Director	**Hiroshi Takahagi**
Technical Manager	**Hisayoshi Shiraga**
Producer	**Minako Naito**
Technical Team	**Takashi Onaka, Saori Okuno**
Company Manager	**Yuki Katsu**
Administration	Phone: 81-3-5391-2115
	Fax: 81-3-5391-2215
	Website: www.geigeki.jp

Tokyo Metropolitan Theatre
1-7-1 Nishiikebukuro Toshima-ku,
Tokyo, 171-0021, Japan

Supported by the Agency for Cultural Affairs, Government of Japan in the fiscal year 2011 for New York and Hong Kong

Tokyo Culture Creation Project

Tokyo Culture Creation Project, organized by the Tokyo Metropolitan Government and the Tokyo Metropolitan Foundation for History and Culture in cooperation with arts organizations and NPOs, aims to establish 'a global culture creation city TOKYO.' The project facilitates involvement of a larger number of people in creation of new culture, by building regional bases for culture creation across the city and offering opportunities for creative experiences to children and young people. Moreover, it creates and globally disseminates new Tokyo culture through organizing international festivals and other diverse events.

NODA MAP

NODA MAP was founded in 1993 and is based in Tokyo, Japan. It is a producing unit, under the artistic direction of writer, director, actor Hideki Noda.

Since 1993, NODA MAP has been producing both large and small scale theatre works with a new creative team and actors each time.

Its productions include *Kill, Pandora's Bell, Oil, Rope, Red Demon* (UK/Japan/Thailand/Korea), *The Bee* (UK/Japan/US/Hong Kong), *The Diver* (UK/Japan), *The Character*, and *South*. The name NODA MAP was inspired by the idea of using the map to guide us from our everyday world through to the land of theatre which is both poetic and physical.

The map is not for tourists but for those who seek cultural synchronicity in order that one day, world theatre will intermingle; not by a superficial knowledge of cultural similarities, but through a deep understanding of cultural differences.

Writer, Director, Actor: **Hideki Noda**
Producer: **Hiroyuki Suzuki**
Web design & Box office: **Aska Kato**
Public Relations: **Noriko Tan**
Administrator: **Yasuko Aoki**

Administration

Phone: 81 3 6802 6681
Fax: 81 3 3468 8027
e-mail: info@nodamap.com
Website: www.nodamap.com

NODA MAP
25-8 Shinsen
#503 Shibuya, Tokyo
150-0045, Japan

Bang in the creative heart of London, Soho Theatre is a major new writing theatre and a writers' development organisation of national significance. With a programme spanning theatre, comedy, cabaret and writers' events and home to a lively bar, Soho Theatre is one of the most vibrant venues on London's cultural scene.

Soho Theatre owns its own Central London venue housing the intimate 150-seat Soho Theatre, our 90-seat Soho Upstairs and our new 1950s New York meets Berliner cabaret space, Soho Downstairs. Under the joint leadership of Soho's Artistic Director Steve Marmion and Executive Director Mark Godfrey, Soho Theatre now welcomes over 100,000 people a year.

'If Marmion's zippy opening production in the main house is anything to go by, there's going to be some punchy new writing to savour.' *Evening Standard*

'Soho Theatre's new basement cabaret space, which has the feel of a comedy club (tables, its own bar) - expect it to become an important room for comedy in the capital.' *Times*

THE TERRACE BAR

Drinks can be taken into the auditorium and are available from the Terrace Bar on the second floor.

SOHO THEATRE ONLINE

Giving you the latest information and previews of upcoming shows, Soho Theatre can be found on facebook, twitter and youtube as well as at sohotheatre.com.

EMAIL INFORMATION LIST

For regular programme updates and offers visit sohotheatre.com

HIRING THE THEATRE

An ideal venue for a variety of events, we have a range of spaces available for hire in the heart of the West End. Meetings, conferences, parties, civil ceremonies, rehearsed readings and showcases with support from our professional theatre team to assist in your events' success. For more information, please see our website sohotheatre.com/hires or to hire space at Soho Theatre, email hires@ sohotheatre.com and to book an event in Soho Theatre Bar, email sohotheatrebar@sohotheatre.

Soho Theatre is supported by: ACE, John Ellerman Foundation, Westminster City Council, Harold Hyam Wingate Foundation

Registered Charity No: 267234

Soho Theatre is supported by Arts Council England and Westminster City Council. This Theatre has the support of the Pearson Playwrights' Scheme sponsored by Pearson plc.

Sponsors
Granta

Principal Supporters
Nicholas Allott
Daniel and Joanna Friel
Jack and Linda Keenan
Amelia and Neil Mendoza
Lady Susie Sainsbury
Carolyn Ward

Corporate Supporters
Cameron Mackintosh Ltd

In-Kind Sponsors
Latham & Watkins LLP
Goodman Derrick LLP
The Groucho Club
SSE Audio
Soundcraft
Nexo

Trusts & Foundations
Andor Charitable Trust
BBC Children in Need
Boris Karloff Charitable Foundation
Bruce Wake Charitable Trust
The Charles Rifkind and Jonathan Levy Charitable Settlement
City Bridge Trust
David and Elaine Potter Foundation
Earmark Trust
8th Earl of Sandwich Memorial Trust
Fenton Arts Trust
Garrick Charitable Trust
Goldsmiths' Company
Harold Hyam Wingate Foundation
Hyde Park Place Estate Charity
John Ellerman Foundation
JP Getty Junior Charitable Trust
Equity Charitable Trust
Eranda Foundation
Mackintosh Foundation
Rose Foundation
Royal Victoria Hall Foundation
Foundation for Sport and the Arts
Sir Siegmund Warburg's Voluntary Settlement
Teale Charitable Trust
The Thistle Trust
Miss Hazel M Wood Charitable Trust

Soho Theatre Best Friends
Miranda Curtis
David Day
Hedley and Fiona Goldberg
Hils Jago, Amused Moose Comedy
Andrew and Jane McManus
Ann Stanton

Soho Theatre Dear Friends
Natalie Bakova
Quentin Bargate
Isobel and Michael Holland
Lynne Kirwin
Sue Robertson
Christopher Yu

Soho Good Friends
Neil and Sarah Brener
David Brooks
Gayle Bryans
Mathew Burkitt
Victoria Carr
Chris Carter
Jeremy Conway
Geoffrey Eagland
Gail & Michael Flesch
James Hogan and Charles Glanville
Alban Gordon
Doug Hawkins
Etan Ilfeld
Jennifer Jacobs
Lorna Klimt
David and Linda Lakhdhir
Amanda Mason
Mr & Mrs Roger Myddelton
Linda O'Callaghan
Alan Pardoe
Tom Schoon and Philippa Moore
Barry Serjent
Nigel Silby
Sharon Eva Degen
Lesley Symons
Dr Sean White
Liz Young

And our supporters who wish to stay anonymous

The text that follows was used for the production at Soho Theatre in February 2012 and was correct at the time of going to press.

Hideki Noda & Colin Teevan

THE BEE

Based on the original story
Mushiriai (*Plucking At Each Other*)
by Yasutaka Tsutsui

OBERON BOOKS
LONDON
WWW.OBERONBOOKS.COM

First published in 2006 by Oberon Books Ltd
521 Caledonian Road, London N7 9RH
Tel: +44 (0) 20 7607 3637 / Fax: +44 (0) 20 7607 3629
e-mail: info@oberonbooks.com
www.oberonbooks.com

Reprinted with revisions in 2011

A catalogue record for this book is available from the British
Library.

ISBN: 978-1-84002-681-8

Cover design by Yuni Yoshida

Printed and bound by CPI Group (UK) Ltd, Croydon, CR0 4YY.

Characters

POLICEMEN

IDO

REPORTERS

DODOYAMA

ANCHOKU

OGORO'S WIFE

OGORO'S SON

OGORO

KING OF CHEFS

The Bee was first performed at Soho Theatre on 21 June 2006 with the following cast:

Tony Bell   Dodoyama, King of Chefs, Reporter
Kathryn Hunter   Ido
Hideki Noda   Ogoro's Wife, Reporter
Glyn Pritchard   Anchoku, Ogoro, Ogoro's Son, Reporter

Director   Hideki Noda
Designer   Miriam Buether
Lighting Designer   Rick Fisher
Sound Designer   Paul Arditti
Assistant Director   Ragga Dahl Johansen
Costume Supervisor   Jackie Orton

Production Manager   Nick Ferguson
Stage Manager   Sarah Buik
Deputy Stage Manager   Hannah Ashwell-Dickinson
Assistant Stage Manager Geraldine Mullins

Head Technician   Nick Blount
Head of Lighting   Christoph Wagner
Technician   Mark Watts

Scenery built and painted by Capital Scenery Ltd.

Soho Theatre Company would like to thank:
Jan and Colin Jamison for the loan of Kathryn Hunter's wig
Richardson Sheffield
Typhoon Europe Limited

The Bee

A residential street in Tokyo, 1974.

IDO
It's been a long day, I make my way home,
Remembering to buy a present for my son.
But as I turn the corner of the street
Imagine my surprise to see…

POLICEMAN
Please keep back, please keep back. The road is closed.

IDO
But I need to get through, I need to get home.

POLICEMAN
Please use another route today.

IDO
That is my home, there is no other way.

POLICEMAN
You mean that house there is your home?

IDO
Yes.

POLICEMAN
You mean that you are Mr Ido?

IDO
Yes I am. Now may I pass?

POLICEMAN
Yes.
No, you must stay here, Mr Ido, you must stay calm,
While I go get Detective Dodoyama.

REPORTERS
Mr. Ido? Did you say that you are Mr Ido?

IDO
Yes.

REPORTER
Ido! It's Ido!

REPORTER
Mr Ido's over here!

REPORTER
July, 1974.
I'm now standing outside Ido's house.

REPORTER
Tell me Mr Ido, tell the viewers how you feel.

IDO
Viewers?

REPORTER
Yes, tell the viewers how you feel.

IDO
I feel…

REPORTER
Yes?

IDO
Surprise.

REPORTER
There it is, you heard it on NHK first.

REPORTER
Surprise? Surprise? Can't you do any better?

IDO
I beg your pardon?

REPORTER
How long have you been married, Mr Ido?

REPORTER
Good one.

REPORTER
You said it.

REPORTER
And repeat the question in your answer,
Saves time with the edit.

IDO
I've been married happily for seven years,
Though there were several years before that when –
Is this about my wife?

REPORTER
You mean you don't know?

REPORTER
He doesn't know.

IDO
Has she done something wrong?
She's not the kind of person who'd commit a crime,
Endanger her own or anyone else's life;
She'd never knowingly do anybody harm,
Do anything that was criminal or even negligent.
She is good and gentle and intelligent
I love her, I love my wife.

REPORTER
Hasn't got a clue.

IDO
My son then, you don't mean it's him?
He's just a boy, barely six, you don't mean,
You couldn't mean, you – ?

REPORTER
He jumps to conclusions faster than we do.

REPORTER
Tell him.

REPORTER
Put him out of his misery.

REPORTER
A prisoner –

IDO
A what?

REPORTER
A prisoner escaped this morning –

REPORTER
He's locked himself inside your house –

REPORTERS
How do you feel now?

IDO
Relieved.

Pause.

But what about my wife and son?

REPORTER
They're hostages.

REPORTER
He has a gun.

REPORTER
How do you feel now, Mr Ido?

REPORTER
Tell the viewers how you feel.

DODOYAMA
Ladies and gentlemen of the press...

The REPORTERS scatter.

Mr Ido, I presume?

IDO
Yes?

DODOYAMA
I am Detective Inspector Dodoyama.
And I think it best for all concerned
That I not, for fear of hurting your feelings,
Sugar the pill, obfuscate the facts,
Beat around the bush, mince my words
Or, in short, prevaricate.
No, I've been in these situations before
And it's best, for all concerned
And, however difficult it might be, to know the score.
So.

IDO
So?

DODOYAMA
Yes.

IDO
Yes?

DODOYAMA
Hmmm.
Earlier today a murderer –

IDO
A murderer?

DODOYAMA
A murderer, by the name of Goro Ogoro,
Escaped from a maximum security prison.
Ogoro, who had been serving twenty years,
Overpowered his guard, took his gun
And shot him through the ear.
Dead.
He then made good his escape.
He wanted to see his wife it seems –
A stolipa at the Hollywood Club.
He'd heard she had another man and wanted a divorce,
Of course Ogoro saw red,
Believing another man to be enjoying the pleasures of his bed.
We knew that he'd make directly for their flat.
We staked it out. He must have seen us.
He eluded our operation
And made instead, by a cunning deviation, for your house
Where he holds your wife and son as hostages
And demand to see his own family, or he'll kill yours dead.
Hey you!

IDO
What?

DODOYAMA
Not you. You!
Don't film so close to the house,
The situation is already delicate.
Ogoro is highly volatile
We don't want to rile him further. So beat it.
Where was I?

IDO
His wife.

DODOYAMA

His wife, yes.
Of course we tried to press her to come here and talk to him,
But she kicked up a right royal fuss.
Would not even listen to us.
Said she's frightened of him.
Besides, today is her son's birthday.
She wanted to stay at home,
To throw him a little birthday tea.

IDO

Today is his son's birthday?

DODOYAMA

Criminals' children can have birthdays just like you and me.

IDO

No, sir, you miss my sense,
I meant that it's my son's birthday too.

DODOYAMA

That, Mr Ido is what we call a –
Yes.

IDO

Coincidence.

DODOYAMA

Yes.

IDO

So how long ago did this occur?

DODOYAMA

Two hours.
When we tracked you to your place of work,
You had gone.

IDO

I had to buy a birthday present for my son.

DODOYAMA

Of course, the birthday, very good.

IDO

A calculator which does mathematics on its own.

DODOYAMA

Ah yes, I believe they're all the rage.
Can't say I understand this modern age.

IDO

You were saying?

DODOYAMA

Was I? No.
You're up to date and up to speed,
You have all the facts you need.
So if that's all –

IDO

But what are you going to do, sir?

DODOYAMA

Do?

IDO

What are your procedures?

DODOYAMA

Procedures?

IDO

You have procedures?
On TV they always say –
My wife says I watch too much,
She says it is my only flaw –

DODOYAMA
This is not TV, Mr Ido, this is reality.
I'm sure I don't have to tell you
That this is a delicate situation –

IDO
You told me.

DODOYAMA
Good. So you understand,
Ogoro is extremely dangerous.
We must proceed with utmost caution.

IDO
But what about my wife and son?

DODOYAMA
I assure you, Mr Ido,
For the time being they are safe.

IDO
You mean they will be in danger later on?

DODOYAMA
I mean that Ogoro has assured us
That he won't touch them 'til later on.

IDO
But he will hurt them then?

DODOYAMA
I am a Detective Inspector, Mr Ido,
I do not indulge in idle speculation.
And please do not worry,
We shall resolve the situation
Before anyone is hurt or maimed or killed.

IDO
Maimed or killed?

DODOYAMA
Don't twist my words.

IDO
But you said 'maimed or killed'.

DODOYAMA
I'm saying not to worry.

IDO
But you said 'maimed or killed'.

DODOYAMA
I'm saying that it won't come to that, most probably.

IDO
Is it possible to speak to this Ogoro then?

DODOYAMA
My men have re-routed your telephone
To our operational H.Q., here.

IDO
Let me speak to him then, persuade him of the advisability
Of being reasonable, giving himself up.
At school I was head of the debating society.

DODOYAMA
Were you indeed?

IDO
I was.

DODOYAMA
There was no such opportunity
To argue the whys and wherefores of an issue
In a debating society at my school.
Nor, I'm sure, did Ogoro's alma mater
Cater for the arts of argumentation

In its various syllabi of education.
In fact, I am convinced that reason and logical argument
Will only serve to infuriate him further
And exacerbate his already considerable natural anger.
And, quite apart from class considerations, he is a stutterer
Which is another source of his antipathy
To anyone who is more articulate than he.
Look at yourself, for goodness' sake,
A well dressed, good-looking man –

IDO
I'm not.

DODOYAMA
You are.

IDO
I'm not.

DODOYAMA
You are.

IDO
Well so what even if I am?
On the phone how would he know
What I look like or how I dress?

DODOYAMA
Your accent.
Ogoro despises the middle classes,
The establishment, the élite, with your comfortable houses,
Your pretty wives, your spoilt son and all your things –

IDO
My son's not spoilt.

DODOYAMA
In Ogoro's embittered, jaundiced eyes he is,

And one call from you with your sound reason
And your logical argument, I'm afraid, Mr Salaryman,
Could send him over the edge.
He'll kill your wife and son on the spot.
And we don't want that do we?

IDO
What are you saying about my accent,
Detective Inspector Dodoyama, sir?

DODOYAMA
I'm saying I always like to look at things
From the criminal's perspective.

IDO
But I am not a member of the establishment, or an élite.

DODOYAMA
I understand the criminal mentality,
I understand the street.

IDO
So you're saying there's nothing I can do?

DODOYAMA
You can, you can trust the police, thank you.

IDO
But you're doing nothing.

DODOYAMA
That's because, Mr. Ido, for the time being,
There's nothing to be done.

REPORTER
Detective Dodoyama, have you come to any conclusion?

REPORTER
Detective Dodoyama, have you any more to say?

DODOYAMA
Yes, ladies and gentlemen of the press,
We have reached a conclusion.
Thank you and good day.

The REPORTERS set up cameras and focus them on IDO. They
assess his performance on a monitor.

REPORTER
So Mr. Ido, how do you feel now?

REPORTER
Now that you know the full story?

IDO
I feel…I feel…I feel sympathy for Mr Ogoro,
As a husband and a father.
At least, I can understand his feelings.
This present here is for my son,
And Mr Ogoro has a son too,
I heard Detective Inspector Dodoyama say,
Whom he hoped to see on his birthday –

REPORTER
Cut!

REPORTER
Good but –

REPORTER
I like the waving of the gift
And the his-son-your-son slant –

REPORTER
We need him to give us more emotion?

REPORTER
To make this work on the evening news
We need some, I don't know –

REPORTER
Anger –

REPORTER
Some shouting –

REPORTER
Even a rant.

REPORTER
Anger,
Shouting,
Rant,
And again.

IDO
I feel sympathy for Mr Ogoro,
As a husband and a father.
At least, I can understand –

REPORTER
Or tears –

REPORTER
Can you do tears?

REPORTER
Yes, do tears. Please.

IDO attempts to cry.

IDO
I'm sorry, I can't do tears.
I feel sympathy for Mr Ogoro –

REPORTER
Most men struggle with the more vulnerable emotions –

REPORTER
So it's a real winner with the ratings.

REPORTER
Come on, come on!

REPORTER
Think pleading –

REPORTER
Think desperation –

REPORTER
Think hysteria –

IDO attempts to portray these contradictory emotions.

IDO
But I am trying to reason with him, gentlemen.

REPORTERS
People don't want reason, they want drama.

REPORTER
We go back and give our producers reason and we're dead.

REPORTER
Come on, do it like he said. Again! 5, 4, 3, 2, 1.

IDO
No, no, leave me alone. Gentlemen
Detective Inspector Dodoyama, sir…?

DODOYAMA
One moment please.
Yes?

IDO
You said that Ogoro's wife won't speak to him.

DODOYAMA
Correct.

IDO

Do you think, if I talked to her, she'd listen to me?
I mean, she must take some responsibility;
I could appeal to her better nature

DODOYAMA

Better nature?
She's a stolipa at the Hollywood Club,
She has no better nature.
But you never know,
It might be worth a go.
Anchoku!

ANCHOKU

Hi!

DODOYAMA

Over here, Anchoku.

ANCHOKU

Hi!

DODOYAMA

I've got a job for you.
This here is Mr Ido, Detective Anchoku,
He wants to see Ogoro's wife.

ANCHOKU

Ogoro's wife?

DODOYAMA

Please take him over there in a car.
Don't worry, it's not far.

ANCHOKU and IDO are pursued by a crush of REPORTERS before escaping into the relative quiet of the car. ANCHOKU produces some food.

REPORTERS
Mr Ido, Mr Ido, tell the viewers how you feel
(repeat)

ANCHOKU
Wait 'til you see her,

IDO
Who?

ANCHOKU
Ogoro's wife, thick as a shit, but on my life,
She's very, very pretty.
Tip-top, A-one, perfect titties.

IDO
Kitty!

ANCHOKU swerves to avoid a cat.

ANCHOKU
What she sees in him, I don't know,
When half of Tokyo would take her out,
Give her a spin.
Know what I mean?
Like Steve McQueen.

ANCHOKU offers IDO some food.

No?
She's a stolipa in some downtown club,
The London or the Hollywood,
One of them.
(*Sings.*) London, London, London, London,
        Tanoshii London,
        Yukaina London,
        London, London!

He laughs, spraying food everywhere.

She can dance for me any day,
Know what I mean?
Tip-top, A-one, perfect titties –

ANCHOKU offers IDO some food.

Perfect, perfect titties but she's thick as shit
You can talk to her all you like,
But there'll be no getting through.
Know what I mean?

IDO
I am beginning to see.

ANCHOKU
Women! Hey, fucking bitches!
Here, why have women got legs?
So they can walk from the bedroom to the kitchen?
Jiggy, jiggy, cook my noodles, do the fucking dishes!
Hi! We're here.

The car stops. It is surrounded by a crush of REPORTERS.
ANCHOKU and IDO attempt to push through them.

REPORTERS
Tell me Mr. Ido, tell the viewers how you feel?

ANCHOKU
Hey you bastards, out of our faces!
We are here on serious business.

REPORTER
What makes you think we're not serious too?

ANCHOKU brandishes his gun.

ANCHOKU
Why don't you tell it to the weapon?
You people should know your places.

IDO
Aren't you supposed to use that with discretion?

ANCHOKU
Do I look like some cop on the beat?
Special branch, my friend, the élite.
(*He strikes a pose.*) like Steve McQueen!

ANCHOKU knocks at the door.

Hello! Anybody at home?

OGORO'S WIFE (*Off.*)
Go away you sons of bitches, go away!
No reporters on my property.

ANCHOKU
We're not reporters, we are the police.

OGORO'S WIFE (*Off.*)
I don't want cops in here either.

ANCHOKU
Well, we're coming in whether you like it
Or whether you like it not.

ANCHOKU and IDO enter the house.

OGORO'S WIFE
I've spoken to you people already today,
I've nothing to add, nothing new to say.

ANCHOKU
Well, this gentleman has something to say to you.

IDO
Madam –

OGORO'S WIFE
Madam?

Who's he and what's he got to say to me?

ANCHOKU
He's Ido, the man whose wife and son
Your psycho of a husband is holding with a gun.

OGORO'S WIFE
What's it to do with me what the son of a bitch does?

ANCHOKU
You are still his wife in the eyes of the law,
And I'm the representative of the law right here, right now.
So hear him out, you stupid cow!

OGORO'S WIFE
Leave me alone, you filthy pig!

ANCHOKU
Whore! You make me want to get sick.

OGORO'S WIFE
Coming into my house uninvited,
Using filthy language in my own home –

ANCHOKU
Filthy home –

OGORO'S WIFE
In front of my own child –

ANCHOKU
Filthy child!

OGORO's WIFE threatens ANCHOKU with a kid's baseball bat that is a present for her SON. IDO intervenes and takes it from her.

IDO
Listen, the two of you, please listen.
Madam, I can see you hate this Mr Ogoro,

But clearly he still loves you.
Is that not the reason he's done what he's done?
That is why I've come,
Can't you see?
Just as your son is dear to you,
So mine is dear to me.
Therefore I ask you, I beg you,
Please talk to your husband.

Pause.

  OGORO'S WIFE
I'm sorry,
I have to make a birthday cake for my son,
Then drop him at my neighbour's,
And then I have to go to work.

Exit OGORO's WIFE.

  ANCHOKU (*To IDO.*)
See what I mean? See what I mean?
(*To OGORO's WIFE.*) Going off to wave your perfect titties
At the yakuza and the salarymen
Who are willing to part with two thousand yen
While this guy's wife and son
Are held at gunpoint by your old man.
You come back and hear him out, you whore, you filthy
   disgusting whore –

*IDO hits ANCHOKU over the head with the baseball bat.
ANCHOKU is out cold.*

Enter OGORO's WIFE.

  OGORO'S WIFE
What have you done? What have you done?

  IDO
Shut up! Shut up!

OGORO'S WIFE
You've killed him! You've killed a cop!

IDO
I have not killed him, I just knocked him out.

IDO removes ANCHOKU's gun from his holster and points it at OGORO's WIFE.

Now take his legs, we'll drag him across the floor.

OGORO'S WIFE
Why?

IDO
To throw him out of your front door.

OGORO'S WIFE
All right, all right, just don't, you know, hurt me.

IDO
Do as I say and I won't. Right, let's go.

IDO and OGORO's WIFE drag the unconscious ANCHOKU outside and return. IDO goes to OGORO's SON and puts the gun against his head.

As long as you do what I say,
I won't hurt your son or you.
Now, close all the windows tight and shutters too,
Put on all the lights.

OGORO's WIFE sets about this, but her SON cries and she goes to him.

Amazing, a slut like you,
And you still love your kid.
Now get on with it, do what I said.

OGORO's WIFE does not move.

Let's see if Mummy, then,
Can close all the windows before we count to ten.

IDO grabs OGORO's SON and puts the gun against his head.
They count:

IDO / OGORO'S SON
One, two, three, four, five, six, eight, nine.

OGORO'S WIFE
Seven.

IDO / OGORO'S SON
Eight, nine, ten.

OGORO's WIFE races around the room closing the windows
and doors.

When she has completed the task, however, they notice that there
is a bee trapped in the room with them. IDO patently does not
like bees. They follow the bee with their eyes around the room. It
eventually alights upon the table. Slowly IDO approaches it with
a cup and then pounces on it. It is trapped in the cup.

Music: Japanese parody of 'The Sabre Dance' by Khatchaturian.
IDO dances.

They are distracted by a ferocious knocking on the door. IDO nods
to OGORO's WIFE and she goes to lock the door. Reluctantly
she passes IDO the key.

IDO
Now, are there any other ways of getting in or out?
Quick, show me about the flat.

OGORO'S WIFE
Left off the entrance hall, the kitchen,
The bathroom facing south,
A six-tatami mat-room,
A storeroom in the rear.

IDO
A beautiful three-sided mirror –

OGORO'S WIFE
What about the mirror?

IDO
It's incongruous, a fine piece like that,
Hanging in place like this,
What's that? On that table?

OGORO'S WIFE
A music box that plays –

IDO
'Swan Lake'.

OGORO'S WIFE
And beside the music box is –

IDO
– the phone.

The phone rings. IDO picks up.

Yes.

REPORTER (*On phone.*)
We want to know what's happening.
There's a policeman here and his head's split and bleeding.

IDO
And who is this I'm talking to?

REPORTER (*On phone.*)
I'm with NHK news.

IDO
I will not talk to you.

REPORTER (*On phone.*)
We have a right to know the truth.

IDO
I repeat, I will not talk to any of you.

IDO puts down the phone.

Security, security!
The windows must now be nailed shut to be quite sure,
Even the tiny one in the storeroom.
The smallest aperture,
Can be a source of weakness.
And remember, if anyone manages to get inside,
Or if you try to run or try to hide,
You and your son will die.
Do you understand the rules?

OGORO'S WIFE
I will go anywhere you want me to.
I will do what you want me to,
I will even speak to him, my husband, Ogoro,
Just please, please let my son go.

IDO
You'll speak to him?
Why did you not say that before?
When I first came to your door,
When I begged you to listen to me?

OGORO'S WIFE
Because now,
Now you have a gun.
Just please, please release my son.

IDO
That, I'm afraid, I simply can't allow.

Don't you see? It's too late now.
And by the way, stop clinging to each other so.
The sight of it makes me want to throw up.

They are interrupted by a noise at the storeroom window. IDO drags OGORO's WIFE into the storeroom.

REPORTER
Hello!

IDO
Hello.
Who are you?

REPORTER
I'm with TBS news.

IDO smacks him in the face with the pistol butt.

Stop, stop, I'm not trying to hurt anyone.

IDO
I know, it's me who is the dangerous one.

IDO smacks him again with the pistol butt.

REPORTER
Why did you do that? I'm on your side.

IDO
Shut up!
You are not on my side.

REPORTER
We just want to know what's going on.

IDO
I told you, I will not talk to you or anyone.

*IDO smacks the REPORTER in the face with the pistol butt.
The REPORTER spits out a mouthful of teeth. IDO fixes the
window closed.*

IDO

Security! Security!

I said windows to be nailed shut!

Back to the living-room, and what do I see?

Ogoro's wife and son trying to sneak out on me.

First they've been crying and clinging to each other,

But, as soon as my back is turned, the mother

Is up and tearing at the door.

IDO points the gun at the ceiling.

IDO

Boom!

The room is shaking.

My ears are ringing.

Mother and child fall to the floor.

They shiver too,

Flakes of plaster are raining down,

But she's up and at the door.

Then go to her,

Hold the gun against her cheek.

(*To OGORO's WIFE.*) This time I shall kill you.

OGORO's WIFE faints. A reporter comes to the letter-box.

REPORTERS (*Off.*)

Hey, what's happening,

What's happening in there?

IDO puts gun through letter-box.

IDO

Stand back, stand back or I shall kill you all!

Back to the centre of the living room.

Get away from the front door!
She's out for the count.
Pull the limp heavy body back into the room –
Now what's this?
He's wet himself.
The little boy has wet himself!
Your child has pissed his pants, woman, change them!

Silence. IDO attempts to change OGORO's SON's pants. The phone rings. IDO continues to play with OGORO's SON, giving him pencils to draw with while he answers the phone.

IDO
Hello?

DODOYAMA (*On phone.*)
Ido?

IDO
Detective Inspector Dodoyama.

DODOYAMA (*On phone.*)
Ido, was it you who knocked Detective Anchoku flat
With a hard blunt instrument believed to be a bat?

IDO
Yes, Detective Inspector Dodoyama, it was me.

DODOYAMA (*On phone.*)
Why did you do that, Ido?
Anchoku is one of my finest men,
Committed to protecting decent society –

IDO
I was a member of that society until quite recently,
But I found I have no aptitude for being a victim.

DODOYAMA (*On phone.*)
But what you're doing is criminal Ido.

Ido, listen to me –

IDO
No, Dodoyama, I'm beyond your jurisdiction now,
You listen to me.
Stand in front of the camera.

DODOYAMA (*On phone.*)
I beg your pardon?

IDO
The camera for the early evening news,
I want to see you.

DODOYAMA (*On phone.*)
Ido, I'm not taking orders from you.

IDO
I have a gun! Dodoyama, just do it! OK?

DODOYAMA (*On phone.*)
Right, then, as you say.

DODOYAMA appears on television.

IDO
Nice to see you again, Detective Inspector Dodoyama.

DODOYAMA (*On phone on TV.*)
Yes.
Hmmm.
Tell me Ido, what am I to do?
Two hostage situations, two locations, two criminals,
But each with the other's family.
This one's not in the manual.
Tell me, is it one case or two?

IDO
Two situations, just the one case.

DODOYAMA (*On phone on TV.*)
And do you seriously hope to save your family like this?
Is saving your family no longer your priority?

IDO
Detective Dodoyama, I'm afraid you don't understand –

DODOYAMA (*On phone on TV.*)
I understand, I do…
I understand, I think…
But tell me, Ido, what shall I do?

IDO
You still have a direct line to my house?

DODOYAMA (*On phone on TV.*)
Yes.

IDO
And one to here now, let me guess.

DODOYAMA (*On phone on TV.*)
Hmmm.

IDO
Put me through to Ogoro.

DODOYAMA (*On phone on TV.*)
Ido, please –

IDO
What is it Dodoyama? Are you all right?

DODOYAMA (*On phone on TV.*)
Yes. No. I don't know.
Perhaps there is something wrong with me,
But you have shirked your responsibility to your family –

IDO
By which you mean?

DODOYAMA (*On phone on TV.*)
I mean that if you argue with Ogoro on the phone,
He might become angry, go for your wife and son.

IDO
What makes you think I'll argue with him?
Do you think I'm not capable of negotiating
Without quarrelling?
What's more, aren't you forgetting,
I've got Ogoro's wife and son here with me?
I might become angry,
I might go for them.

DODOYAMA (*On phone on TV.*)
Is that a threat?

IDO
What do you think?
Would you like me to threaten you?
Would that make life easier for you?

Pause.

DODOYAMA (*On phone on TV.*)
Hmmm. Yes.

IDO
In that case, it's a threat!

DODOYAMA (*On phone on TV.*)
In that case, you leave me no choice.
Give me a few minutes to patch the lines through.
Do you mind if we listen in to you?

IDO
Surely you're going to whatever I say!

DODOYAMA (*On phone on TV.*)
I'm just trying to be polite.

IDO

It's about time you showed me some respect.

DODOYAMA (*On phone on TV.*)

Two situations, one case,

I must be going insane.

Tell me Ido what should I do?

IDO

I would watch myself, Dodoyama, if I were you,

Someone might be listening in to you, too.

IDO puts phone down and notices that OGORO's WIFE is trying to pull down the hitched up hem of her dress.

(*To OGORO's WIFE.*) Hey you! The game is up. Besides,

A stolipa should be used to showing a bit of thigh.

IDO kicks OGORO's WIFE.

Go nail the storeroom window shut, if you please.

OGORO's WIFE complies.

Phone rings. IDO answers it. As he does so OGORO, standing in IDO's front room, answers a phone at the same time.

OGORO

Wh…wh…who is this?

IDO

I should ask you, you rang me.

OGORO

Y.…y…you rang me, what do you m…m…mean?

IDO

Wow! They weren't joking about that stutter!

OGORO (*On phone.*)

Wh…wh…wh…!

IDO

Forget it. They probably rang us at the same time,
When they patched the two lines together.
So, you're Ogoro?

OGORO

Y…y….y…

IDO

Yes.
And that is my house that you're standing in.
I'm Ido.
Your hostages are my wife and son.

OGORO

Wh…wh…wh…?

IDO

So I am now with your family,
Here boy, it's Daddy.

OGORO's SON takes phone. He might make a noise but does not speak before OGORO's WIFE grabs it from him.

OGORO'S WIFE

You son of a bitch, you son of a bitch!
What are you doing with this man's son and wife?
Why are you doing this to me?
You are ruining my life.

OGORO

But I l…l…love you –

OGORO'S WIFE

I hate you!

OGORO

You are my w…w…wife –

OGORO'S WIFE
Putting us in danger, you son of a bitch!
You stupid, stupid piece of shit!
He's got a gun.

OGORO
I've got a g…g…gun too you know.

OGORO'S WIFE
Why did you break out of prison?
What possessed you?

OGORO
Because of the d…d…divorce.

OGORO'S WIFE
What divorce?

OGORO
Because of the other m…m…man.

OGORO'S WIFE
What other man?

OGORO
I heard w…w…word.

OGORO'S WIFE
Not from me, you stupid son of a bitch, not from me.
Is that what this is all about?
There is no divorce, there is no other man,
Except this one standing here with a gun.
So, leave his house, give yourself up, go back to prison,
Say that it was all a mistake, a crime of passion.

OGORO
I c…c…can't. I k…k…killed a guard.

OGORO'S WIFE
You what?

OGORO
You heard.

OGORO'S WIFE
You stupid, stupid, stupid son of a bitch!
I should divorce you.
Get out of that man's house, leave his family –

IDO takes the phone from OGORO's WIFE.

IDO
So there you have it, the state of affairs.
Where do you think we should go from here?

OGORO
It's my s…s…son's b…b…birthday,
L…l…let me talk to him.

IDO
It's my son's birthday too.
First tell me what did you get for him?

OGORO
A c….calculator.

IDO
Fancy that. How did you get hold of it?

OGORO
I stole it, didn't I?

IDO
Of course you did. Of course you did.
Listen, listen! Ogoro. Let's do a deal;
You give my son what you got yours.
I'll give your son what I got mine in return.

OGORO

Wh....wh...what did you get yours?

IDO

A calculator.

OGORO

What make?

IDO

Casio.

OGORO

Casio? Casio? I Never heard of them. You think...
I'm not going to g...g...give my son some second rate junk.
Think you can cut it as a cr...cr...criminal?
Ido, your d...d...deal-making ability is ab...ab...abysmal.

IDO smashes up the present. OGORO does the same.

IDO

Well to hell with you too and to hell with your wife and son.

OGORO

Wh...wh...what are you going to do with them?

IDO

Nothing if you leave my house.

OGORO

If I leave your house, they'll send me b....b...back.
And I won't see her,
And she's the reason that I've done what I've done –

IDO

Don't you get it? She doesn't want to see you.

OGORO

S...s...so there is someone else, s...someone new?

IDO

Come over here and ask her yourself.

OGORO

No, you b…b…bring my family here to me.

IDO

No, you leave,
Or, though I have always considered myself a pacifist,
I shall rape your wife and kill your son.

OGORO

H…h…how can you say such a thing?
Y…y…you want to be a r…r…rapist Ido? and a murderer?

IDO

No, I am a businessman, Ogoro, at heart,
A ruthless businessman.
And you're going to see how ruthless
A ruthless businessman can be.

OGORO

D…d…don't touch her.

IDO

If you leave my house, I'll leave them alone –

OGORO

I can't.

IDO

That is the deal, if not…

IDO stalks OGORO's WIFE along the floor. She attempts to preserve her modesty.

– the rest I leave to your imaginations.

IDO turns on the television; there is a cookery programme.

KING OF CHEFS (*On TV.*)
– thanks Bob.
And as for those of you who have not the patience
To prepare the traditional meal,
Here's something else, something simpler,
Something you can eat sitting on the sofa,
Off a plate on your knees –

IDO
I'm hungry.

KING OF CHEFS (*On TV.*)
Sit down in front of the TV –

IDO
I'm hungry, did you not hear me?
I said I'm hungry.
It's nearly seven thirty.
I always have my dinner by this time,

KING OF CHEFS (*On TV.*)
A nice romantic evening in.

IDO
And my wife is a good cook.
Chicken teriyaki is her speciality.
So stop snivelling and get cooking.

OGORO'S WIFE
But I'm meant to be at work by eight.
We get docked if we are late.

IDO
You don't feel like preparing my meal?

OGORO'S WIFE
I'm not as good as your wife, I'm sure.

IDO

I'm sure you're not either.

Right, go then. Go to your club,

Have fun.

Just don't be surprised if, when you get home –

IDO takes the key out of his pocket, unlocks the front door and pushes OGORO's WIFE out of the house.

You find that I have barbecued and eaten your son.

KING OF CHEFS (*On TV.*)

– the rest I leave to your imaginations.

Pause. OGORO's WIFE knocks on the door. IDO opens it.

OGORO'S WIFE

Perhaps I shall stay home tonight, after all.

IDO

I think you've made the right decision.

IDO leads her to the kitchen and stabs a chopping knife into the chopping board.

KING OF CHEFS (*On TV.*)

A nice romantic evening in.

The phone rings. IDO turns down the TV and picks up the phone. Both the TV CHEF and OGORO's WIFE are chopping in the background.

OGORO

I...I...Ido?

IDO

Ogoro.

OGORO

H...h...how is my wife, Ido?

IDO

Cooking.

OGORO

Wh…wh…what do you mean?

IDO

I'm hungry, so she's cooking me a meal.

OGORO

And th…th…then?

IDO

We'll eat.

OGORO

T…t…together, like a f…f…family?

IDO

Yes. Watching TV.

OGORO

Then w…w…we'll eat together too.

Pause.

Wh…wh…what then?

IDO

Bed, I guess.

OGORO

The s…s…same or d…d…different beds?

IDO

Same. Don't want them to escape.

OGORO

N…n…no.

IDO

But don't worry,

I won't have your wife 'til later.
That's the deal.

OGORO
What d...d ...deal?

IDO
The deal, Ogoro.
If by morning you're not gone,
I'll rape your wife and hurt your son.

OGORO
Wh...wh...who's the fucking criminal here, me or you?
Aren't you f...f...forgetting I have your wife too?

IDO
No.

OGORO
Then y...y...you bring me my wife and son or I'll h...h...
    hurt yours.

IDO
You don't want to exacerbate
My considerable natural anger, Ogoro.

OGORO
Or wh...wh...what?

IDO
Who knows what I could do,
Now that I'm the same as you?
Look at your son's small white arm...
Such a shame to do it harm!

OGORO
Wh...wh...what could you do? What could you do?
Y...y...you don't have the balls.

IDO
I don't have the balls?

IDO twists OGORO's SON's arm. SON screams.

OGORO
Wh...wh...what are you doing? What's going on?
Wh...wh...what are you doing there to my son?

IDO
And next I'm going to strangle him.

OGORO
Stop it, stop it p...p...please.
P...p...please leave him alone, p...p...please

IDO
What kind of criminal p...p...pleads with his victim?

OGORO
Now y...y...you've asked for it.
I'm g...g...going to beat up your little shit.

OGORO's WIFE arrives with music box. All except IDO scream, howl, etc. An abrupt silence. Only the sound of the music box playing 'Swan Lake' continues.

IDO
And over the melody of 'Swan Lake',
I heard my son screaming for help
And my wife trying to restrain Ogoro.

The music stops. A finger snaps. Such is IDO's distraction that he does not notice.

OGORO
Wh...wh...what was that noise?
Wh...wh...what have you done?

IDO

I seem to have broken the little finger of your son.

Music: KING OF CHEFS sings 'My Way' in Japanese.

OGORO's SON rolls around in agony. OGORO's WIFE rolls around in sympathy. IDO puts down the phone. End of musical interlude.

IDO sits and watches television while OGORO's WIFE, hysterical, sees to her SON, bandaging his finger and administering him painkillers. Telephone rings. IDO picks it up.

Yes?

DODOYAMA (*On phone.*)
Ido, turn over to NHK.

IDO does so.

DODOYAMA (*On phone on TV.*)
Ido, I want you to be able to see me,
To see how angry your actions have made me – ?

IDO turns down the volume on the TV and listens on the phone for a few moments.

IDO
Yes Dodoyama, it is broken.

He listens.

What? Is that a threat?
Do not dare threaten me,
Or I am liable to get very angry.

He listens.

A doctor? I cannot admit a doctor
How could I be sure he was not an impostor?
A policeman in disguise?

He listens.

Now, I want to eat and watch TV.
Good night, Detective Inspector Dodoyama.

IDO hangs up.

Where's my dinner? I want it now!

OGORO's WIFE fetches their dinner. IDO changes channel on the TV. The volume is still turned down.

IDO
And, as I eat, I begin to relax,
I reflect on all that has happened, all that has passed,
I begin to feel that I am more in control
Than any time previously in my life;
That I am growing accustomed to my new role.
As I said before, I'd no aptitude for being a victim,
And that is why I have decided
To step outside, go the way of the criminal.
Imagine my surprise to see
That this, this was the true me,
And being me was now my main responsibility.
Now I am alive,
Alive to how things really are,
Alive to all the possibilities.

IDO raises a cup to OGORO's WIFE. She fills it.

Kampai!

IDO lifts another cup so that she might drink too, but this is the cup that contains the bee. The bee flies around the room and lands on IDO's face. It crawls over his face. His eyes demand OGORO's WIFE help, but she is torn. At length she goes to his aid. The bee flies off. IDO follows it with his gun. He takes a shot. Silence.

The bee appears to be dead. Music: Japanese parody of 'The Sabre Dance' by Khatchaturian. IDO dances and encourages OGORO's WIFE to do her club routine. As she dances IDO deliberately puts the gun on the table and goes to the mirror to straighten his tie. Once again OGORO's WIFE is torn. Tentatively she reaches for the gun. She even manages to point it at IDO, but she can't shoot. She has chosen to be a victim. She puts it down.

IDO is aware of this, he turns. He goes to her and leads her to bed. OGORO's SON joins them. They lie down. IDO, roused by the song, tosses and turns and cannot sleep.

What day is it today?

OGORO'S WIFE
Thursday.

IDO
Thursday's the day I make love to my wife.

OGORO'S WIFE
But you said not 'til tomorrow morning,
On the phone to him, I heard.

IDO
I also said that I'm now a criminal,
And a criminal does not have to keep his word.

IDO attempts to part her legs. Twice she resists. The third time she acquiesces.

She does not offer much resistance
To my advances or physical insistence.
And it only adds to my thrill
The thought that my own wife is, at this same time,
Being raped by Ogoro, against her will.

IDO ejaculates.

I ejaculate almost immediately,

And then we go to sleep.

Music: the humming chorus from 'Madame Butterfly'.

The next morning. IDO rises and goes about his routine of shaving and straightening his tie while OGORO's WIFE irons his jacket, just as if this were his home and this were a normal day. He goes to the table where he is joined by OGORO's SON and is served breakfast by OGORO's WIFE. They eat. IDO picks up the phone. The music stops.

Ogoro?

DODOYAMA (*On phone.*)
It's me, Ido.

IDO
Dodoyama?

DODOYAMA (*On phone.*)
I thought it most unwise
To let you criminals continue to talk
And so rise to the other's provocation.

IDO
I see. And am I to surmise from that
That he's still in my house?

DODOYAMA (*On phone.*)
Hmmmm.

IDO
Have a policeman go –
No better, you yourself go,
And stand below the storeroom window.
I have a gift I want you to take to Ogoro.

IDO puts down the phone. He goes to the kitchen and returns with a knife and chopping board.

You must excuse me, how rude I am,
But in all the confusion, I forgot to ask the little man
His name.
Come here and tell me what your name is, boy.

OGORO'S WIFE
Rokuro.

IDO
Rokuro. And what age are you Rokuro?

OGORO'S WIFE
He was six yesterday.

IDO
Six. Big boy, same age as my own.

IDO takes knife.

Well Rokuro, I'm sad to say the deadline,
The one I set your father, has been and gone,
And he has not yet left my home.
So now, I'm afraid, my little man,
I must remove the little finger from your hand.

IDO cuts off the SON's broken little finger. OGORO's SON faints.
OGORO's WIFE screams. IDO drains the blood from the finger.

Envelope! I need an envelope!

Beside herself with horror, OGORO's WIFE obediently fetches
an envelope. IDO makes her put the finger in the envelope.
He then addresses it and goes to the storeroom window where
DODOYAMA waits.

DODOYAMA
Ido, I really think –

IDO shuts the window.
The phone rings. We see DODOYAMA on the TV screen.

DODOYAMA (*Barely coherent with rage.*)
A finger! Ido, a finger?
You a salaryman? You should know better.

IDO is not interested and turns down the sound while DODOYAMA lets off steam. When he has calmed down he turns the volume back up.

IDO
Just hand it over to Ogoro, or else…

DODOYAMA
Or else what?

IDO
Or else who knows what I could do, Dodoyama…

DODOYAMA
Is that a threat?

IDO
That's a threat, Dodoyama. Happy?

DODOYAMA
Happy.

IDO
Good.

IDO puts the phone down. He turns up TV. A REPORTER is on TV.

REPORTER (*On TV.*)
I'm now standing outside Ogoro's wife's house,
Where the gruesome package has just been handed out,
The same gruesome package which is now in transit to
Ogoro to be handed over.

IDO goes to letter-box and shoots the REPORTER.

He shot me! I repeat, he's shot me
The bastard shot me!

*The shot has woken OGORO's SON who writhes around like a
prawn on the grill. OGORO's WIFE is hysterical. She tries to
give her son more painkillers but they don't calm him.*

*DODOYAMA delivers a different coloured envelope through the
letter-box. IDO goes to it and opens it. It contains a finger. It is
the finger of Ido's son.*

*IDO stands a moment, then goes to OGORO's SON and takes
him in his arms.*

  IDO
Once upon a time there was a man
Who, for all the world, appeared to be good.
He worked hard, cared for his family,
And lived life as it is commonly felt that one should.
But one day a bad man came into the good man's life,
And took as hostages the good man's son and wife,
And for all that the good man was good,
He could not bring himself to behave
As it is commonly felt that one should.
So he made the decision to become perfectly bad
To out-bad the baddie in the bad tricks that he had.
This was what he had to do, he knew that he should.
And the badder he got, the more it was good.

*IDO cuts the ring-finger off OGORO's SON's hand. IDO drains
the blood from the finger.*

 I need a envelope!

*OGORO's WIFE, switching from hysteria to insane calm retrieves
an envelope and puts the finger in it. IDO goes to the bathroom
window and delivers it to DODOYAMA.*

*When he returns to the room, OGORO's WIFE leads him to
the bed.*

Music: the humming chorus from 'Madame Butterfly'.

They awake the next morning. Their daily routine now becomes a ritual that is performed in ever decreasing circles. The ritual consists of the following:

They rise.

IDO shaves, straightens tie, goes to the table where OGORO's WIFE helps him into his freshly ironed jacket then fetches the breakfast which they eat.

After breakfast IDO cuts off another of OGORO's SON's fingers. IDO delivers this to DODOYAMA who, upstage, performs his own ritual of finger delivery.

IDO is then led to bed by OGORO's WIFE who straddles him, has sex with him, and then they go to sleep.

On the second circuit, OGORO's WIFE has a moment of sanity before breakfast where she is struck by the horror of the situation, but OGORO penetrates her from behind which distracts her. This breakfast sex becomes part of the ritual.

On the third circuit, OGORO's SON dies.

On the fourth circuit of the routine, as IDO prepares to cut off one of OGORO's WIFE's fingers over breakfast, he asks:

IDO

And as I about to cut the ring finger,
I linger with the knife
I cannot tell this is mine or Ogoro's wife.
Who are you?

He cuts off her finger, places it in an envelope and delivers it to DODOYAMA at the storeroom window. This time, as he has sex with OGORO's WIFE he removes four more fingers. She sinks to the floor and dies. He places the four fingers in an envelope and is about to hand them to DODOYAMA through the window.

IDO
And gradually the world around me fades,
The media finds a new story, the police a new case.
Just one lone policeman, Dodoyama, remains,
He comes around once a day
To convey mine and Ogoro's gifts.

IDO hands over the four fingers and lethargically sets off on a new circuit. However, there is no more food. There are no more fingers. He picks up the phone.

Ogoro?
Ogoro, you still there?
You see Ogoro I faced you down
And now, now I'll send my own finger round.

IDO puts down the phone and is about to cut off his own finger when he hears the bee.

WWW.OBERONBOOKS.COM